Parent/Teacher:

A Simultaneous Role

Parent/Teacher:

A Simultaneous Role

by
Maurice J. Butler, M.Ed.

To my wife - Cassandra, my daughter - Dominique,
my brothers: Malvin, Kevin, Edgar III, Christopher,
William and In Loving Memory: my mother - Clara,
my father - Edgar, my sister – Karen
and my niece - Kevanna

Preface

As a classroom teacher, one has the opportunity to view, firsthand, the interactions between parents and their children. This includes many instances that range from dropping children off at the door to assisting them with their homework and the many interactions in between.

Whether children are living with one parent or both parents, a dual role must be assumed. Such a role includes acting as both a parent and a teacher. While this role may be quite challenging at times, parents must continue to move forward with all due diligence.

The role of a child's parent is a responsibility that has to be acknowledged. Once again, this role is combined with the function of also acting as the child's first teacher. Introducing your child to the wonderful world of learning begins in the home before his first day of school.

Table of Contents

Chapter 8

Chapter 9

Chapter 10

Introduction

Having worked as a public school teacher for a number of years, I have had an opportunity to observe many instances that involved teachable moments concerning the lives of children. My insistence that they receive a quality education is closely related to any parent wanting the best for her child.

If a quality education is the ultimate goal, parents must assume a proactive role in the home as they prepare for the journey of educating their children.

Parent/Teacher: A Simultaneous Role contains the author's commentary and his examples of family related stories based on the points raised throughout this book. Each insight reveals the author's feelings of scenarios consistent with possible interactions between parents and their children.

1

A Parent's Role & the First Steps

A child's desire to learn must begin in the home before his first day of school. This desire will require a number of things that facilitate learning so its transfer from home to school is as rewarding as possible.

The parent is the first to assist her child with the beginning of the wonderful world of learning. Given this, she is considered her child's first teacher. She may want to begin with the fundamentals. A child who learns how to write his name, recognize and pronounce each letter of the alphabet correctly, count and recognize numbers 1 to 50 is well on his way to preparedness for kindergarten.

◆ • • • • • • • • • • • • ◆

Ms. Johnson decides she wants her son to learn how to write his name before he enters kindergarten.

"Joey, will you come and join me at the kitchen table?"

Three year old Joey puts down his toy car and walks just a few feet to meet his mom in the kitchen. His mother motions him over to the chair where a sheet of paper and a pencil are waiting for him. Joey climbs up onto the chair.

"Alright, son, I'm going to teach you how to write your name."

Mom takes the bright red pencil and places it into Joey's hand. She takes her hand and places it around her son's hand. She moves the pencil up and down, left to right, while forming each letter as carefully as she can. She repeats this procedure three more times.

"Okay, Joey, I want you to try it for mommy."

Joey's mom hands him the pencil. Joey begins to write the first letter of his name followed by the other three. His mother picks up the paper, and sings praises to her son.

"What a good job, you've done, Joey! I'm so proud of you!"

Speaking positively to your child paves the way for further advancement. A parent should never utter words that are of a negative nor degrading nature, as such utterances do nothing more than create a sense of despondency for your child. We must always speak life or respond with positive commentary to our children.

A child can point out the various letters of the alphabet as he and his mom walk down the cereal aisle of the grocery store.

For example, "Look mom, the letters on that cereal box are big C-o-r-n, big F-l-a-k-e- and s."

"Very good, Joey! The letters spell Corn Flakes."

This is just one example of how the interaction between parent and child allows for the familiarity of the alphabet to eventually become second nature. Such a pattern between parent and child must be consistent, as repetition is the key to success. Also, learning how to pronounce each letter of the alphabet can promote the proper pronunciation of unfamiliar words at the kindergarten level.

◆•••••••••••◆

The twins, Erin and Eric, were playing with their Legos in the middle of the living room floor.

"I want to make a tall building," said Erin, as Mr. and Mrs. Taylor sat watching their four year old twins from the sofa.

"I think she's going to be an architect," said the twins' dad. All of a sudden, Eric scooped up a bunch of pieces and began to arrange them in the shape of a simple stethoscope.

"You know Eric was asking questions about the doctor's stethoscope while we were at the pediatrician's office yesterday. He seemed really fascinated with it. Maybe he'll be a family doctor," said mom.

The Taylors realize that an educational journey of a thousand miles begins with a single learning experience between parent and child. They decide that the best way to begin helping their children fulfill their dreams is to provide them a running start. Prior to enrollment into school, they believe the basics present the best way to begin.

"Hey twins," called their dad. "Come on over here. I want to talk to you." Erin and Eric dropped the Legos, and walked over to the sofa.

"You know kids, this fall; one of the first things your teacher will start teaching is counting. She will teach your class how to count to 50. So, your mom and I thought it would be a good idea if you learned how to count before your first day of school."

Together, the twins looked at each other and said, "Okay, dad."

"Alright children," said mom, "I'm going to count to ten using sticks of gum." Mrs. Taylor took a pack of gum out of her purse, and placed each stick on the table in front of her children, as she counted.

"One, two, three…ten." After counting to ten, the twins' Mom said, "Okay kids, this time, I want you to try counting with me."

The twins' mom started out "One, two,…" The twins joined their mom, and they all stopped at ten.

"Very good, kids. Alright, this time I'm going to count to twenty." Mrs. Taylor repeated the same process for the numbers eleven to twenty with ten more sticks of gum. The twins counted with their mom from eleven to twenty.

"Very good, guys," said their dad.

"What number did we stop at, Erin?"
"TWENTY!" shouted Erin.

"Good!" exclaimed her mom.

"So, how many sticks of gum are there, Eric?"

"TWENTY!" exclaimed Eric.

"Very good, son! Alright Eric, I want you to separate these sticks of gum by two's," said his dad.

"What does that mean, dad?"

"It means you're going to separate them like this." The twins' dad began separating the sticks into three stacks with two sticks of gum in each stack.

"Alright, Eric, did you see what I did?" Eric nodded his head.

"Okay, now you separate the rest of them. You may use the whole table. I want you to keep going until all of the sticks of gum are in stacks of two just like these three stacks."

Eric began to do as his dad had asked by stacking two sticks of gum on top of each other until all of the sticks had disappeared from the pile.

"Now, Erin," said her mom. "How many stacks of gum do you see?" Erin began to count the miniature stacks of gum.

"I see ten stacks," mom.

"Great job, Erin! You both did a good job," said their dad.

"Okay," said the twins' dad. "Let's see how you do with our family photo album." Mr. Taylor pulled out the photo album from underneath the coffee table, and showed the children pictures taken of a family reunion right after the twins were born.

"Alright, let's see how many people are in this picture. On the count of three, let's begin," said dad.

"One, two, three . . .," said the twins as they joined in with their dad. "Four, five,...,"

Mr. Taylor stopped counting, and the twins kept going.

"Six, seven, eight, nine, ten, eleven, twelve," said Erin and Eric.

"How many people are in the picture?" asked mom.

"There are twelve people in this picture," said Erin, as her brother sat gazing at the pictures.

"Good answer!" said Mrs. Taylor.

"Since you both did really well with counting, your mom and I are going to take you to get some ice cream," said dad.

"Yeahhhhh…," said the twins.

The family's SUV backs out of the driveway. "What flavor ice cream would you kids like?" asked the twins' dad as he turned the corner.

"I want vanilla," said Eric.

"I want Superman," said Erin.

"We can go to the Dairy Queen. It's only six blocks away," said the children's mom.

"Alright, how many scoops would you both like?" asked dad.

"TWO scoops, please!" said the twins.

"I tell you what, guys; let's get some more practice with counting. But, we'll make it even more fun. Erin, I want you to count the street signs on your side until we get to the DQ. Your dad will keep count. Eric, I want you to count the street signs on your side until we get to the ice cream parlor, and I will keep count. Whoever gets the right answer will get two scoops of their favorite flavor," said mom, as the twins' dad stopped at the first light.

"I see a sign!" said Erin.

Mr. Taylor drove two more blocks, as the

children continued counting street signs.

"I see two!" said Eric. Several signs later, the family reached the DQ.

"Alright, Erin, how many did you count?" asked her dad.

"I counted five."

"You're right, Erin," said her dad.

"Okay, Eric, how many did you count?" asked mom.

"I counted seven signs."

"Well, Eric," said his mother. "I counted eight signs. I'm afraid your sister will get two scoops."

"I'm glad one of us got an extra scoop," said Eric as he hugged his sister.

Teaching your children how to count can be related to people they come in contact with, the number of rose petals on a rose, the number of slices in an apple pie, the number of students in their class, or the number of birthday invitations to send out.

An introduction to counting numbers should include everyday activities so that this much needed skill can be viewed as fun rather than as a chore for your child. Learning can be fun. Also, children need to see that learning various concepts can be linked.

For example, given the previous scenario, Mr. and Mrs. Taylor can extend the counting activities when the family returns home. The mother could explain the concept of addition by asking the twins to put the numbers, they came up with, together to see how many there are in total. She could go on to explain that the concept of subtraction includes taking the smallest number of street signs from the largest number.

2

Guidance Is Key

From the moment a child is born, he begins to bond with his parents. It is at this exact moment parents realize their desire to be all they can be to support their child. A proud mom and dad prepare for many responsibilities that will serve to promote much happiness for their family.

One of these responsibilities includes educating their children prior to starting school and from this point going forward. As stated in the previous chapter, it's more beneficial to work with your child prior to entering the kindergarten.

A firm understanding of the fundamentals, as your child enters school for the first time, certainly cuts down the amount of anxiety children typically experience entering school or an environment, for the first time, quite different from their home.

For example, once the teacher begins a lesson on "Counting Numbers," a child who has already been exposed to this concept by his mother and father will be able to master the lesson given this thorough introduction by his parents.

The process of teaching your child prior to the start of school should continue even after he's started school. In doing so, a foundation for teachable moments between parent and child will become routine for the child. He may even look forward to sessions after school that involve homework.

These interactions, however, should not be limited to homework, but they should also include a review of the concepts the teacher is working on. If you are not comfortable reviewing a particular concept with your child, it would be in your child's best interest to consider researching the concept on the Internet in the presence of your child. The Internet has a wealth of information that can explain virtually any concept taught at the K – 12 grade levels.

This practice can serve two purposes. It shows your child how committed you are to assisting him with understanding the lesson. This can be considered a 'moment of bonding.' Secondly, it enables your child to report to school, the following day, with the confidence of having a better understanding of what his parents have shown him.

At the beginning of the school year, some teachers will accommodate parents with an extensive list of concepts they intend to teach for the entire year. Given this, parents can actually assist their child with concepts prior to its introduction by the teacher. Now, you might say, "What if some parents don't have the time to stay ahead of the teacher based on the parent's work schedule or other commitments?" I guess it comes down to a matter of deciding which priority will be more beneficial in the long run.

A parent who chooses to place her child's

success in school above other matters is going to reap the benefits when her child is someday in a position to take care of her mom and dad in their later years. This luxury stems from the very first time mom and dad taught their children how to count to twenty when they were all in front of a television set that was not on.

Children are very observant. They emulate what they see adults doing. In order to ensure children refrain from unwanted behavior, they must be given guidelines to follow and examples to model from the moment they realize that their immediate environment is one that can be explored and mishandled.

Children are given boundaries they must adhere to. Teenagers, on the other hand, may ignore such boundaries their parents attempt to set. This may be due, in large part, to parents having waited far too late to set parameters for their children, or teenagers to follow.

Teenagers who do as they please were not given the guided tour between the ages of five and ten with respect to consequences that were far more sober than "no dessert after supper."

Starting at the sixth grade, students, of this description, will continue to ignore authority figures or teachers. Such defiance will cause their grades to suffer because they have been inadvertently given the green light to do as they please.

However, all is not lost. The reestablishment of a partnership between the parent and the teacher will provide the answers to steering this group on the right path again. If teachers can point out the things that can be done at home by providing parents with a blueprint to assist their teenagers with academics, the parent is now in a position to play the role of the teacher so that their children are able to be successful in class.

Teenagers, who are not focused on their studies, will find other interests in which to engage. Teenagers want structure. They want someone to be firm with boundaries that must be set, as they are actually afraid to commit to mischief. But, having succumbed to peer pressure, they feel there is no other alternative.

◆• • • • • • • • • • • •◆

There are varying views on parenting. Some believe it's okay to reward their children for getting good grades. Others view going to a party with their teenager as a way to connect with their child.

Ms. Peterson rewards her daughter, Julia, with a new cellphone for getting all "A's" on her report card.

"I'm so proud of you, Julia," said her mom.

"I really wanted the cellphone you promised me if I got good grades on my report card," said Julia. "I can't wait until school starts in the fall!"

When Julia goes back to school in the fall, she is going to do all she can to get a new wardrobe for Christmas. Her eagerness to start school in the fall may be considered the right response. But, it's for the wrong reason. While a parent should be pleased that her child is eager to return to school, an eagerness to return should not be based on being rewarded to do so.

This type of reward system sends the wrong message to a child. Julia is not attending school for an education alone. She is simply going to class and making excellent grades in order to be rewarded by her mother. The focus has shifted from acquiring knowledge and a skillset to receiving tangible goods that are only temporal.

One might ask, "Well, why can't she be doing both?" I don't know that a student can fully absorb the material in class to be used later on in life if she doesn't have the right motive to begin with.

Secondly, this approach suggests a child will always want to get something in return for completing a task. Isn't it better for a child to have a sense of integrity compared to a desire to always please self when it results in a distorted view of morality?

A sense of integrity must be entertained. Continuing to reward your children for success they achieve, every single time they do so, is not the way to introduce this concept. Integrity is a characteristic that can be taught. For example, if you and your child are aware that your neighbor is taking packages from the doorstep of others in the area, as the parent, you could provide the police with an anonymous tip in the presence of your child.

Or, you and your child are walking out the grocery store, and you say, "Oh, my! That cashier gave me twenty-five cents too much in change."

"Oh, mom, it's only twenty-five cents!" exclaims your daughter.

You immediately take your daughter by the hand, and you walk back into the store to return the money.

◆••••••••••••◆

Parenting can also be confused with an

attempt to bond by engaging in activities consistent with the younger crowd.

"I'll see you later, dad," yells Mike.

As Mr. Evans' son leaves out the back door, his dad hurries down the stairs.

"Hold on, son. Where are you going?"

"Me and the fellas are going to watch the game at The Garden."

"Why didn't you say so? I'll get my hat." Mike's dad hurried to the hall closet.

"I guess next time, I'll just have to sneak out," thought Mike. He didn't want to tell his dad he wasn't happy with him always wanting to follow him whenever he goes out with his friends.

Bonding with your child is a matter of spending time with him and not with his friends. Because Mike's dad wants to constantly try and be a part of his son's life by sharing his time with he and his friends, Mike has grown to resent this interference. Since he chooses not to hurt his father's feelings, he decides to sneak out of the house the next time he and his friends plan an outing.

A child who feels he must sneak out of the house to keep his parents from accompanying him can obviously lead to great harm for the child. A parent must know where to draw the line. This lets your child know you can trust him to choose the right friends.

Now, one might wonder if this was a matter of Mr. Evans wanting to bond with his son, or was he trying to learn more about his son's friends? There has to be a separation of the two, so as not to have your children sneaking out of the house. If you want to meet with your child's friends, invite them over to the house. Don't crash their little get together.

◆•••••••••••◆

"Hey girl, did you get your email about an invite to Melissa's party?"

"I sure did!" shouted Jennifer.

"Okay, then I guess I'll see you on Saturday, Maria," said Jennifer. As Jennifer hung up the phone, her mom walked into her daughter's bedroom.

"Is everything okay, Jen?"

"Yeah, mom, Maria and I are going to hang out on Saturday."

"Oh! Where are you guys going?"

"We're going to Melissa's seventeenth birthday party on Saturday." Mrs. Eccleson responds with a smile.

"What are you smiling about?" asked her daughter.

"I'm just thinking about the new dress I bought yesterday at Lenore's. I could probably wear it."

"Wear it to where?" asked Jen.

"To Melissa's birthday party, of course," said Jennifer's mom.

"But, mom, the email I received plainly states 'by invitation only...' "

"Well, I'll just take you to the party, and hang around until Melissa's mom asks me to have a seat."

"Okay," said Jennifer, as she walked away with a look of despair.

"We'll have a good time!" said her mom.

Is it really okay for a parent to hang out with her daughter as if they are best friends? Once again, the wrong message is being sent to the child. Parents must assume the role of the adult who monitors behavior from afar if their seventeen year old was given permission to attend a birthday party. The parent must remember, in most cases, there is adult supervision at the party. If you are in doubt, you can always call ahead to make sure.

We must also ask "Is Jennifer's mom trying to monitor her daughter's behavior or bond with her?" If you say she's trying to bond with her, this is probably not the best way to go about it. If you say she's trying to keep an eye on her, this is also not a good idea.

Again, bonding should be an event shared with your son or daughter and not with the sons and daughters of others. Monitoring your child's behavior by riding along with her to a party and staying afterwards suggests that your child probably thinks you don't trust her.

3

A Few Learning Specifics

Many teachable moments that have enormously impacted a child who enters the classroom for the first time and moving forward imply that his parents were quite creative. Parents realize they have to be creative in order to assist the teacher in her efforts to educate their child. Even though the parent is considered the child's first teacher, establishing a partnership with the teacher does not negate this fact.

If a child struggles to read, a parent will buy books, or borrow books from the library to assist the teacher with teaching her child to read. Once a child can see that you are willing to go the extra mile to ensure his success, he will be even more interested in wanting to sail that hurdle and ultimately achieve success with reading.

Teaching your child how to count, or how to read is important. But, teaching your child how to dress himself is just as important. I can recall a child who came to school wanting his teacher to put his shirt on him because his teacher noticed he was wearing it on the wrong side.

◆ • • • • • • • • • • • • ◆

Ms. Thompson dropped her dry erase marker on the floor near Roger's desk. Wanting to be so helpful, the first grader reached down and picked up the marker. He handed it to his teacher.

"Thank you, Roger." Mrs. Thompson walked over to her desk. "Roger, would you come up here, please?" Roger walked to where his teacher was sitting.

"Roger, I want you to go into the boys' room, and turn your undershirt on the right side."

"But, Ms. Thompson, I don't know how to put my shirt on the right side."

Despite being stunned at Roger's remark, Ms. Thompson simply asked him to return to his seat.

One might wonder why Roger doesn't know how to properly dress himself. This can only be the result of his mom or dad not taking the time to teach him. It probably goes without saying, but mom and dad need to take out the time to teach their children how to properly dress themselves, and not allow children to take care of this skill set alone.

While putting on a shirt may be considered a simple task, it's not so much a matter of teaching the skill itself, but rather it's the idea of bonding with your child while teaching him at the same time. Bonding with your child is not confined to the engagement of fun filled activities.

◆•••••••••••◆

Your child's learning environment at home sets the tone for successful one on one 'teachable moments.' On the other hand, if there are a number of toys in a child's room, or other rooms in the house, you may not have your child's full attention despite the fact that she is not actually playing with the toys.

Allison's dad had a short work day, and decided to pick her up from school. The two entered the house and walked into the kitchen.

"You two are just in time for dinner," said Mrs. Robertson.

After washing their hands, Allison and her dad sat at the kitchen table. Mrs. Robertson had not been home long before she was able to put something together for her family.

Minutes later, "Okay, sweetheart, it's time to do your homework," said her dad. Allison ran upstairs to get her homework, and ran back downstairs into the kitchen.

"Daddy, can we do my homework in the big room?"

"Sure, sweetheart, we can go into the family room." As the two walked out of the kitchen, and into the family room, Allison's dad stumbled over one of her dolls.

"I'm sorry, daddy."

Allison walked over and picked up her doll and placed it into the toy box in the corner of the room.

"Okay, let's see what you have for homework, Honey." Allison took out her reading book, and her homework paper.

"According to your homework paper, it looks like you have to read this story and answer three questions."

Mr. Robertson knew he had to help his five year old daughter with some of the words.

"Alright, Allison, begin reading."

Allison was looking at the doll she placed in her toy box.

"Go ahead, Allison. Start with the first word."

Allison began reading. "As Mr. Jones was walking his dog, a great big…."

"German Shepherd," said her dad.

"Okay, Allison, continue."

"German Shepherd broke away from him," said Allison. "It started running down the street. Mr. Jones ran after his dog. He stopped in front of the…"

All of a sudden, Allison's doll fell from the shelf of her toy box. She jumped up and walked over to place her doll back on the shelf.

◆ • • • • • • • • • • • • ◆

"Alright, young man, let's get started on your homework," said Mrs. Williams, as she closes the kitchen door that leads to the garage.

Marcus needs a little help with two digit addition. The second grader sets his book-bag onto the kitchen chair.

"Okay, son, let's go into the living room and get started." Marcus grabs his book-bag and follows his mom. He takes out his math book and homework.

"Let's look at the first one, Marcus. I want you to watch me."

His mom takes his homework paper. She also takes out a sheet of scratch paper and a pencil from her husband's desk.

"Nine plus eight is seventeen. But, I can't write down both the one and the seven. So, I'll write down the first number and regroup the next."

After explaining and modeling the word regroup, mom completes the problem, and shows her son three more from his homework paper.

"Okay, son, I want you to try number five."

Marcus begins writing. He follows the diagram his mom made as she explained the steps to solve the problem.

"I'm finished, mom!" says Marcus smiling,

"Good job, son! You did very well."

"Can I have a cookie, mommy?"

"Yes, you may, but just one. I don't want you to spoil your dinner. I want you to try and finish your homework before dinner."

Marcus took his homework into the kitchen to finish it while eating his cookie.

While both of these scenarios yielded different learning expectations or outcomes, they both are examples of parents wanting to assist their children with homework after school. Allison was seated in an area where her toys occupied a portion of the room. Given her fascination with her doll, she was not able to focus on any instruction from her dad. As a result, her dad was not able to accomplish anything with his daughter.

On the other hand, Marcus completed his homework in two areas including the living room and the kitchen. Both rooms were free of his toys or obvious distractions that can prevent learning. As a result of Marcus' ability to focus on the instructions of his mom, he was able to do well on his homework.

Do you suppose Allison's dad agreed to work in the family room because he wanted his daughter to be in a relaxed environment or at least in an area where she is most comfortable? There may be some merit to this strategy. But, if a room of this type is used to do homework with your child, it's best you insist your child focus and adhere to your directions.

Parents who wholeheartedly want their children to succeed in school believe in buying into the educational process for the sake of their children's learning. They understand that they must assist their child's teacher by working with their child at home. A child, who receives an understanding of various concepts from his parents at home, and his teacher in school, can expect to become a well-rounded learner.

A child who has a parent spending moment

after moment teaching him those things that are introduced in school can easily see that his mom or dad wants him to become successful. However, along with a parent's desire to teach her child how to read, write, add and subtract, for example, she must also make sure she has her child's undivided attention while working through these concepts.

This, as we have seen with Marcus, can best be accomplished by choosing an area in the home that has the least distractions or no distractions at all. This leaves your child with nothing other than to focus on your instruction and the lesson.

◆••••••••••••◆

Ms. Cooper was considered an over-achiever throughout her K-12 and collegiate educational experience. She recalls having been purpose driven in order to make the grade. She went on to become quite successful in the business world. Her endeavor is to make sure her son is, at the very least, just as successful.

"Jeremy, I want you to create five more two digit addition problems similar to the ones we've just worked together," said his mom.

"Aw mom, I just finished writing a short story about a lost puppy."

"I know you did, son, but I want to provide you with as much practice as I can with writing compositions."

Jeremy began to write his problems.

Minutes later, "I'm finished, mom," he yelled.

Ms. Cooper walked into her son's room just as he was reaching for his bat and baseball glove.

"Just a minute, young man, let me check your answers to those problems."

"It looks like you got four right and one wrong. Now you have to do twice as many as these. How many is that?" she asked.

"Ten," said Jeremy in a disappointing tone.

"Okay, have a seat, son," said his mom as she pulled his chair out from his desk, and motioned him to sit.

Ten minutes have gone by, and Jeremy's mom peaks her head in.

"How are you doing, son? Is everything okay?"

Jeremy's mom chose not to assist him this second time around because she wants him to have the confidence to achieve on his own.

"I have one more," said Jeremy.

Upon finishing the problem, he walked over to where his mom was sitting.

"Here you are, mom."

"Great job, son! I knew you could do it," said his mother after checking his answers.

"Now, let's prepare for another English lesson. The story you wrote was good, but I want you to be even more prepared for the math and English lessons Ms. Green is going to teach your class next month."

Ms. Green has already given her parents a list of the monthly concepts she intends to teach for the school year.

"Awww, mom, that's so far away," cried Jeremy.

"Remember what I said, son. It's always best to be somewhat prepared for the work your teacher presents to the class."

Jeremy was so tired. He simply didn't want to do anymore. But, he didn't know how to tell his mother he was beginning to dislike working so much.

Time management regarding the rate at which a parent insists that her child constantly engulf himself into learning can affect his desire to learn. It reminds me of the old saying, "All work and no play makes Jeremy a dull boy." A parent, who chooses to stay ahead of the game by teaching beyond what the teacher is currently working on, may cause a child to gradually lose interest.

I can certainly appreciate a parent wanting her child to excel in school. But, as you have just read, a rigorous episode of bombarding your child with one academic task after the other, without a break of any kind, can ultimately result in a lack of enthusiasm for learning.

When Jeremy reached for his bat and glove, this should have been an indication to his mom that he wanted to do something else. Parents must always listen and observe the flares their children send up. These signals help to paint pictures.

Often times, children don't know how to verbally express themselves. So, they use alternative ways in which to communicate with their parents. When a baby cries, he is letting mom know he's hungry, wet, or simply irritable about something. His mom immediately tries to determine exactly why her baby is crying. If a

mother can immediately attend to a baby's need,
then why not the cares or wants of a third grader?

4

A Child's Curiosity Is Essential

"Look, mommy, pretty pink flowers sticking up out of the snow!"

Ms. Monroe reached down to pick up a flower her daughter was so intrigued with. The two were taking a walk through the park on a brisk, snowy December morning.

"Honey, this is called an annual." Eight year old Megan took the flower from her mom, and put it to her nose.

"Okay, Sweetheart, it's time to go home."

"Okay," said Megan as she tried to stuff the flower into her coat pocket.

"No, Megan, don't do that."

Megan's mom opened her purse, and Megan

gently tucked the flower inside.

Mrs. Monroe and her daughter arrived back at the apartment shortly after noon.

"Megan, dear, can you come into the kitchen, please?"

As Megan walked over to the sink, where her mother was standing, her mother was reaching into the cabinet to get a small vase.

"I know what you're getting ready to do," said Megan.

"Yes, honey, I'm going to put our little flower into the vase. I want you to hold the vase under the faucet, and fill it with water until the water is almost to the top."

Megan took the vase and filled it with water. She had seen her mom do this a number of times. Children can strengthen their sense of recall through witnessing a series of repeated events.

"Mommy, how can flowers grow during the winter? I can see why they grow in the spring and summer because that's what they do during this time of the year."

"Well, Megan, these flowers are called Annuals. They're called Annuals because it takes a whole year for these flowers to form stems, leaves, and petals."

"Oh, and since December is at the end of the year, it's going to take a whole year for this flower to do all of this," said Megan.

"Very good!" said her mother.

"Mommy, can we look at some more pictures of these flowers on the computer?"

"We sure can."

Megan's mom took out her laptop and placed it on the kitchen table. She did a Google search and in less than five seconds, a beautiful array of purple and pink flowers sprouted on the screen.

"Ooooo, mommy! How did you do that?"

"It's called surfing or looking on the Internet using Google."

"What's Google?" asked Megan.

"Google is a website that allows us to find out a lot of things. Someday, your teacher will teach you how to use the Internet to look up some things for an assignment."

"But, mommy, why can't you teach me?"

"Alright, Sweetheart, let's look up the different kinds of Annuals." Megan's mom places her daughter's fingers on the keyboard.

"Okay, Honey, type the words *kinds of Annual flowers*, and let's see what comes up."

Megan searched for the letter 'k' on the keyboard, and continued tapping a key for each letter until she typed each word.

"Okay, Megan, now tap the key that spells ENTER."

Megan searched around the keyboard and said, "Here it is!" She tapped the Enter key and pictures of beautiful flowers popped up on the screen.

"Mommy, is this all I have to do when I want to look up something on the Internet?"

"Yes, Megan, but for right now, the Internet is only to be used for research."

"What's research?" asked Megan.

"Research is a matter of looking up information for a certain topic."

"Oh, okay. So, when I want to research a topic, I can just use your laptop. Right, Mommy?"

"No, not unless we look up your topic together," said Megan's mom, as she closed the lid to the laptop and put it back in her office.

I like the way Megan's mom taught her daughter how to use the laptop for the purpose of using the Internet. Her mom also used good judgement in the way she handled her daughter's question regarding use of her mom's laptop for research. While this is a learning tool or excellent way to introduce the world of technology to your child, it must be a supervised teachable moment.

Now the question remains, "At what age should a parent allow their children to surf the Internet?" Certainly it is a personal choice, but allowing your child to use the Internet unsupervised comes with a price – trust. Parents, who allow their teenagers to hang out with friends without parental supervision, should use the same judgement with respect to trust and use of the Internet. Children, obviously, have to wait about ten years to surf the Internet unsupervised.

Learning can certainly be a fun time for

children. They begin to explore the world around them. Their curiosity is the starting point at which they begin to wonder. This sense of wonder about the things around them is the beginning of learning.

◆••••••••••••◆

Three year old Jason climbed up onto the chair at the dining room table. All of a sudden, "CRASH!" A glass bowl fell on the hardwood floor. Mr. Everett came running into the room. He picked up his son to make sure he was okay.

"Are you alright, son?"

As Mr. Everett sat Jason in the chair, his son smiled reaching for his dad's beard. Mrs. Everett came running down the stairs.

"Jason, where are you?"

"He's fine, dear."

Taking Jason by the hand, Mr. Everett walked into the kitchen.

Jason's mom hurried into the kitchen, and took one look at her son. She picked him up and walked into the dining room.

"Oh, noooo…, my beautiful glass bowl."

Mrs. Everett looked at her son, "What am I going to do with you? How many times have I asked you not to climb up onto the chairs in the dining room," said Jason's mom as she sat him in the chair. Seconds later, his dad picked him up.

"I wish you wouldn't do that while I am trying to remind our son about not climbing onto chairs," said Jason's mom.

Since toddlers have a tendency to explore the world about them, make attempts to conquer it in their own way and to have a need or desire to make a conquest, parents must be willing to allow for this interaction by their children. If certain items are in the path of a child's road to discovery, simply remove the items in order that you are not faced with having to scold your children. A reprimand has the potential for stunting a child's curiosity.

While every child needs a set of boundaries that must be followed, why not simply do all that you can to minimize the likelihood that your child will bring harm to himself or others. As another saying goes, "An ounce of prevention is worth a pound of cure."

◆••••••••••••◆

"Daddy, why do birds build nests so high up in the trees, or on the inside of the roof of the garage?" asked Rudy.

Rudy saw a bird outside of the kitchen window fluttering back and forth from the window sill to a tree in his backyard.

"Those are very good questions, son," said Mr. Foster. "What do you say we use my cellphone to find the answers to those questions?"

"Your cellphone!" said Rudy in a surprised tone.

"Yes, son, a cell phone is actually a mini computer. As an insurance salesman, I have to use my computer at work to find out answers to all kinds of questions. Well, this little cellphone can do a lot of the same things my computer at work can do. Look here," said Rudy's dad as the two walked to the living room. "All I have to do is tap this key here." Rudy's dad showed him the key. "I would also add, while speaking into the phone, 'Why do birds build nests so high up in the trees'?"

While his dad's phone is trying to respond, Rudy thinks for a moment, as he tries to figure it out.

"I know dad," said Rudy.

"So, what do you think, son?"

"I think it's because the momma bird wants to keep her baby birds away from animals."

Rudy's dad reads what is typed on the phone to his son. "It says birds do what they can to get as far away from other animals. Your answer is just as good as this one, son."

Children can learn by doing some child-like analysis on their own and in their own way. For example, when it was suggested that birds do what they can to get as far away from other animals as they can, Rudy remembered that his dog was jumping up and down in front of the tree, as a bird was flying around it. An ability to see, and determine how a piece of the puzzle fits, is an excellent beginning for children.

Also, recall, if you will, where Rudy and his dad were sitting when his dad decided how they would discover the answers to Rudy's questions. Even though they were in front of the television, which was showing Rudy's favorite cartoon, he was still interested in the habits of birds.

Children love to ask questions about their environment. This is how they begin to put it all together concerning what makes the wheels on a tricycle go round and round for example. For a child to be more concerned with why birds do what they do instead of watching a cartoon on television suggest his parents have exposed him to a number of far more interesting things.

The constant interaction with nature is the best way for children to gain a real sense of their environment as opposed to simply having someone explain it to them. Interaction is far more interesting than listening all of the time.

5

Children Are Like Sponges

It's often said that the minds of children are like sponges. They can memorize many details through rote learning, or the ability to recall through repetition. They also try and model what they see and hear. They can do a good job of learning a second language, for example, because their young minds are not filled with so many other things.

Ms. Wilson pulled into the driveway. Andrew jumped out, counting the steps, as he ran straight to the refrigerator once he was inside.

"Hold it, young man," said Andrew's mother. "You know you have to wash your hands after you walk in the door!"

Andrew walked to the bathroom to wash his hands. He reappeared and sat at the table where his mom had placed one cookie and just a little milk.

"Did anything special happen in school today?" asked Andrew's mom.

"Ms. Stevens gave us a poem that has eighteen lines. She said we have one week to memorize it."

"Well, after dinner, you and I will sit down and try to memorize your poem together."

"Do you have to memorize it too, mom?"

"No, son, I'm going to show you how to memorize a poem."

Mr. Wilson walked into the kitchen just as Mrs. Wilson was putting the cornbread into the oven. Andrew came running into the kitchen.

"Hi, dad!" said Andrew hugging his father.

"Hello, son, how was school?"

"My teacher said I have to know a poem by next Thursday."

"I'm sure when the time comes for you to say every line of the poem in front of the class, you'll do just fine."

"In front of the class!" said Andrew as he stood with his mouth wide open.

"Don't worry, son. It'll be alright," said Andrew's dad, as he gave his son a hug.

"Alright let's sit down and eat," said Mrs. Wilson.

About one half hour later, "Okay, let's see your poem," said Andrew's mom. After taking his poem out of his backpack, Andrew walked into his room.

"Have a seat at your desk, son." Andrew's mom sat in a chair next to her son.

"Okay, Andrew, I want you to repeat the

first three lines after me." Andrew did as his mom had asked. He and his mom repeated this pattern until the entire poem was read three times.

"Now, Andrew, I want you to read the first three lines. After that, I want you to look up at the ceiling and say the same three lines without looking at your paper."

"Okay, mom," said Andrew as he began reading and reciting.

"Very good, son," said his mom. "Now, I want you to read the next three lines of the poem, and then repeat them by saying them out loud."

Andrew began to read and repeat the next three lines.

"Okay, son that's enough. We'll memorize some more tomorrow. I want you to brush your teeth and get ready for bed."

"Okay, mommy," said Andrew while putting

toothpaste on his toothbrush.

Andrew went on to memorize the entire poem in a week. When Ms. Stevens called him up to the front of the room, he did an excellent job for a first grader. She said if you weren't watching him, and just listening, you would automatically assume he was reading the poem instead of reciting it from memory. I find this utterly fascinating given Andrew is in the first grade.

◆ • • • • • • • • • • • ◆

Just as children have the ability to memorize sentences, they also have the capacity to memorize phrases commonly spoken under certain conditions. Social graces, such as saying 'please and thank you,' should be taught to children at an early age. Children can memorize these phrases by simply hearing their parents saying them over and over. A time will come where mommy and daddy won't have to remind their children of these gracious gestures.

Preparation for in-school and National

Spelling Bees is also evidence that children have an overwhelming ability to memorize or recall.

"Mommy, mommy, I can spell it!" said little seven year old Jacob. "I really want to win that contest."

"Are you sure, you can spell it, son? Spaghetti is a pretty big word."

Jacob and his mom were doing a mock Spelling Bee in Jacob's room. Mrs. Cooper was preparing her son for his Second Grade Spelling Bee. Two weeks of practicing with his mom had gone by, and Jacob felt he was ready for the Bee.

"Today is the big day, son. Are you sure you're ready."

"Yes, mom, I'm sure," said Jacob, as he placed his notebook into his bookbag.

"Did you practice anymore after we practiced together?"

"No, mom, I was tired."

After a grueling three rounds of spelling one word after the other, it was finally announced that Jacob Cooper was the Second Grade Spelling Bee Champion for the Emerson Elementary school.

"Mom, mom, I won, I won," said Jacob as he ran to his mother in the audience.

"Hi, dad, when did you get here?" Jacob's dad picked him up and gave him a big hug.

"I left work a little early. I couldn't miss this for anything in the world," said Jacob's dad.

"Okay, everyone, the performance is over," said the principal. "I'd like to thank everyone for coming out this afternoon."

"Alright, you two, let's go home. I'll fix us some lunch," said Mrs. Cooper.

Investing time into your child's interest in a

Spelling Bee, for example, can certainly pay off. Anytime a child can become really excited about school, half the battle is won. This would be a good time to build upon this interest by letting your child know he can accomplish anything as long as he is willing to work and put forth the effort.

◆•••••••••••◆

"Parlez-vous Français?" (*Do you speak French?*) A foreign language can be challenging for adults to learn. "What about children?" While adults can learn a foreign language in a given amount of time, it unfortunately takes us longer to master it than a child.

"Bonjour classe! Robert, fermez la porte, s'il –vous plait." *("Good morning, class! Robert, close the door, please.")*

Ms. Duval often speaks to her class in French. They can catch on to the previous request she asked of Robert because she repeats the same phrase to him every morning he walks in late, leaves the door open, and goes back to close it right after Ms. Duval utters this phrase.

As she prepares to teach her third grade students how to count in French, she tells the class to "Répétez apres-moi," *("Repeat after me!")* She goes on to count to ten and says, "Un (one), deux (two), trois (three), quatre (four), cinq (five), six (six), sept (seven), huit (eight), neuf (nine), dix (ten)." Her class repeats each number after their teacher.

Two days later, Ms. Duval decides to pick up the pace since all of her students have mastered the memorization of counting to ten in French, as well as pronouncing the numbers correctly.

"Okay, class, let's move on to some simple greetings."

Ms. Duval takes the class through a few drills. Children can easily learn a foreign language because their minds succumb to learning new material, or simply soak it up like a sponge without worrying about deadlines. It's as if it almost comes natural to them. They're able to learn a foreign language because they view it more as fun, as opposed to viewing it as a conquest or a dire need to learn the language. Adults, on the other hand, have some difficulty mastering a new language because they are forced to learn it.

◆••••••••••◆

"Say Jane, where are you and your husband planning to go this summer? I know you're probably already looking forward to getting away and not having to worry about all those leaves in your front yard anymore."

"Well, Jen, Mark and I would like to take a trip to Paris, but I can't speak any French at all. Mark took three years of it in college."

"Yes, I've heard him say a little here and there, but I never knew what he was saying," said Jen. "You know, Jane, I signed us both up for French lessons with a tutor. His name is Mr. LeFleur. He has an office downtown near the Rialto theatre. I thought you might want to surprise Mark, some day, when you engage him with a conversation in French."

"When do we start?" asked Jane.

"Mr. LeFleur has agreed to start next Monday."

The following Monday, "Bonjour, Madmoiselle Jen Carter et Madame Jane Smith, dit Monsieur LeFleur." (*Hello, Miss. Jen Carter and Mrs. Jane Smith, said Mr. LeFleur.*)

"Bonjour, means hello. If you noticed, I referred to one of you as Madmoiselle and the other as Madame. Mademoiselle is for a woman not married, and Madame is for a woman who is married," said Mr. LeFleur.

"Uh, Bonjour," said Jane and Jen together.

"I understand that you simply want to be able to carry on everyday conversation in French, and not master anything beyond this. I also understand that you want to try and accomplish this by next summer. Let's see, this is October…What month do you want to actually be able to carry on a conversation in French?"

"How's the middle of July?" asked Jane.

"Okay, I'll do what I can. Nous allons commencer," (*Let's begin*) said Mr. LeFleur.

"Whenever, I say Répétez apres-moi that means Repeat after me."

"Bonjour, monsieur!" said Mr. Le Fleur.

"Bonjour, monsieur," said Jane.

"Tout le monde!" said Mr. LeFleur.

"This means everyone," said Mr. Le Fleur.

Jen was staring at the word Mr. LeFleur had written on the smartboard, and trying to pronounce it.

"Ladies, for right now, let's simply listen to

the sounds of the words rather than trying to pronounce them."

"Let's try it again, together, with a different phrase. Comment-allez-vous?" (*How are you?*)

"Répétez apres-moi," Jane and Jen repeat the phrase.

"Comment-allez-vous?"

"It means, how are you? Now, try Je vais bien. This means I am well," said Mr. LeFleur. Jane and Jen repeat this phrase.

"Okay, try this one. Comment-allez-vous, madame? This means – How are you, madame?"

Jane and Jen repeat this phrase.

"Can we try to hold a conversation with each other? I know we've only learned a couple of phrases," said Jen.

"Who wants to start?" asked Mr. LeFleur.

"Bonjour, Jane! Comment-allez-vous?" said Jen.

"Je vais bien," said Jane.

"Comment-allez-vous, Jen?" asked Jane.

"Je vais bien," said Jen.

"Alright, ladies, I want both of you to take this booklet home, and practice saying more phrases that are outlined in the booklet," said Mr. LeFleur. "Tell you what, why don't you two study pages four through twenty, and be ready to have another conversation based on these pages. Let's meet again next week." Jane and Jen walk out of the classroom.

"Did you see the number of phrases there are within those pages?" asked Jane.

"Well, if you want to get this done by next summer, we had better get started. Why don't we meet tomorrow at your house?" said Jen.

The next morning, "Come on in, Jen. Have a seat," said Jane.

"What is all of this?" asked Jen.

"These are the things that are going to speed the process along. This tape recorder will allow us to listen in order to hear how we sound. These workbooks will help us translate sentences written in French to English," said Jane.

"Okay let's get started," said Jen.

"That's enough. I think we're ready for Mr. LeFleur," said Jane after the two completed five hours of studying, and holding a mock conversation between each other.

"If you say so," said Jen.

"What do you mean?" asked Jane.

"I'm not sure if I'm ready," said Jen.

"Why don't you think you're ready?" asked

Jane.

"I'm just not remembering things the way I could when I was a lot younger," said Jen.

"I'm sure Mr. Le Fleur doesn't expect us to be perfect. Just do the best you can, and I'll see you tomorrow," said Jane.

The next day, "Alright, ladies, have you been studying and familiarizing yourselves with the many phrases listed on pages four through twenty?" asked Mr. LeFleur.

"We have, but I have a question," said Jen.

"Alright, Madmoiselle Carter, what's your question?"

"I'm not sure I can learn at the pace you are taking us. My sense of recall isn't what it used to be. Is there any way you can take us at a much slower pace?" asked Jen. "My third grader is taking French, and he does a lot better than me. I want to be able to help him, but I need to learn as much as I can."

"How do you feel about that Madame Smith?" asked Mr. LeFleur.

"Well as my friend said, maybe you shouldn't give us so much at one time. My sense of recall is okay, but certainly not enough to acquaint myself with so many French phrases all at once."

"Well, ladies, I'm afraid unless you're willing to familiarize yourself with the material I ask you to study, I can't help you. Good day!"

"That's it?" asked Jane.

"You're not going to even try and convince us that we can do this?" asked Jen.

"The only way we can move forward is if you are willing to invest the time for these lessons," said Mr. LeFleur.

"There must be another way, Mr. LeFleur,"

said Jen. "Once again, based on my limited recall, I will need an alternative way to learn a foreign language," said Jen.

"Then, I'm afraid I can't help you. I've already stated my position. Good day ladies!"

Mr. LeFleur returned to his desk, and appeared as though he was preparing for his next client. Jane and Jen walked out of his office.

Some adults can find learning a new language somewhat challenging. I suppose if you have been accustomed to speaking one language your entire life, it would be somewhat difficult to learn a new language.

If you want to help your child, as he navigates his way to learning a foreign language, and you are not proficient in this area, you can still help your child by encouraging him that he can master another language.

Trying too hard or forcing yourself to learn a foreign language because you are trying to accomplish a goal could hinder your chance to master it. It's no longer seen as fun, which is why English speaking children are able to learn French easily. Unlike adults, they don't feel the sense of urgency.

6

Life's Lessons

A famous mathematician, Sir Isaac Newton, once said, "For every action, there is an equal and opposite reaction that must occur." Children who fail to listen to mom or dad may have to pay the price. But, the price doesn't necessarily mean something negative. On the contrary, if a professional basketball player scored fifty points, he was able to break his personal scoring average for one night despite the fact that his team lost the game.

◆••••••••••◆

As Abigail settles down to sleep, she hears her collie barking loudly in the backyard. She thinks nothing of it because Charlie is always barking at the blue jays that fly in and out of Mr. Adams' birdhouse next door.

"Roof, roof, Roof!"

"Stop that barking," yelled nine year old Abigail, as she pulls her head back into the window.

The next morning, Allison went to the window to call Charlie, as she does every morning. "Charlie, Charlie," she called.

"Hmmm....He usually comes running out of his doghouse. I better go see what's going on," she thought.

Allison gets dressed and in minutes, she's looking inside and outside of Charlie's doghouse, "Charlie, Charlie!" she called.

All of a sudden a gust of wind blows the back gate open.

"Oh, no, I left the gate open!" says Allison, as she watches the gate swing back and forth. She runs into the house right past her mom who was putting dishes into the cupboard.

"Mommy, mommy," cried Abigail. "I guess

I forgot to lock the back gate last night because Charlie's gone."

"I'm in here, Sweetheart. Are you sure you didn't lock the gate?" asked Abigail's mom. "Maybe a strong gust of wind blew it open."

"Let's see, I went out last night about 6:00 o'clock to take Charlie for a walk…Oh, no! I think I forgot to lock the gate after I got back from taking Charlie for a walk."

"Abigail, how many times have I asked you to always remember to lock the gate after you return from taking Charlie for a walk? Let's wait a day to see if Charlie returns. He's done this before. Don't you remember? Last month you left the gate unlocked when you and your friends returned from entering Charlie in a contest for the most beautiful coat in the neighborhood."

"I remember mom. I just wish I could remember to always lock the gate," said Abigail as she walked into the living room and flopped on the couch.

"Honey, how many times have I asked you not to flop on the couch?"

"I'm sorry, mom. I'm just upset."

"I know you are, Abigail. Tomorrow, you and I will go through the neighborhood and post signs on trees letting people know that our Charlie is missing."

The next day, the glow and warmth of the sun was shining brightly on Abigail's face.

"What a bummer," she thought as she awoke to the first day of her summer vacation. "At least, I'll get plenty of exercise when mom and I post signs all over the neighborhood that spell out the words 'LOST DOG – PLEASE PHONE RIGHT AWAY IF FOUND.' "

Upon walking downstairs, the smell of pancakes cooking lured Abigail right into the kitchen.

"Good morning, Honey. In honor of your

first day of your summer vacation, I thought I would make your favorite smiley face pancakes with butter and hot maple syrup."

"Thanks, mom, I am hungry. But, I just wish I knew where Charlie ran off to. I already thought about what to write on the signs we're going to use."

"That's good, Sweetheart. But, you need to eat breakfast before we go out. I have already called the office and told the staff that I was taking the day off."

"I wish dad was here," said Allison as she poured syrup on her pancakes.

"Well, he won't be back in town until this weekend. Besides, if he was here, you would probably hear him tell you the same thing I did."

"I know, and I will have two parents who are upset with me."

"Honey, I'm not upset with you, and your

dad would not be upset either. We all make mistakes including me, your dad and a whole lot of other people," said Abigail's mom, as she leaned over to hug her. "Your dad and I simply want you to try and be more responsible by remembering the things we ask you to do."

All of a sudden, there was quite a bit of barking in the backyard. Abigail ran quickly to the window and then out the back door. She leaned down and gave Charlie the biggest hug ever, as she waved to her mom in the window.

◆••••••••••••◆

"Dad, I'm not sure I have the right answer, but here it is."

"Okay, son, let's see what you came up with."

Todd's dad is an algebra teacher at Stevenson Middle School. He and his son are working on some algebra homework. Todd has a test on Friday.

"Well, son, it looks like you still don't quite understand how to find the unknown in this equation. Let's look at it one more time because it's getting late, and you have school tomorrow. I want you to be wide awake in my class." Todd and his dad try the problem together.

"Son, you have to pay attention to what you're doing," said Todd's dad calmly. "The slightest mistake can throw the whole equation off. You go on up to bed. We still have two days before the test on Friday."

After dinner, the next day, Todd and his dad sit down at the table in his dad's study to try and solve some more equations.

"Okay, son let's go back to the beginning. As I stated in class, you must begin every equation this way." Todd's dad shows him how the equation should be solved.

Todd was trying to hang on to his dad's every word, but he was too busy paying attention to the cell phone on his lap. He had just received a text message from his girlfriend.

"I'm going to create an equation, and rather than ask you to solve it on your own, I want you to tell me what to do first."

Todd thought for a moment, "You have to ask the question, what are you trying to solve?"

"What do you do next?" asked Todd's dad as he wrote his son's comments on his legal pad.

"You must write down the unknown letter with an equal sign and the answer. Alright go ahead and finish solving the equation. "

"That's enough, son," said Todd's dad after looking at his son's answer. "You may go on up to bed?"

As Todd jumped up from the chair, excited about the text, and finally having a chance to reply, his cellphone hit the hardwood floor. Mr. Stevenson looked down at the floor, and picked up the cellphone.

"Is this why you were not able to understand the things I was saying?" Todd didn't know how to respond.

"I'm waiting!" said Todd's dad in a rather angry tone.

"Well, dad, I just don't understand algebra. So, I focus on something that I'm more interested in."

"Okay, son, we'll talk tomorrow."

"Two more days before the test," thought Todd, as he rolled out of bed. "What am I going to do?"

He finished getting dressed, and walked downstairs. On his way to the kitchen, he remembered to get his calculator from his dad's study. He walked into his dad's study, and over to his desk. His calculator was right next to the answer sheet to Friday's Algebra Test. Staring at the answer sheet, as he couldn't believe his dad left it on his desk, he turned his head. Todd picked up his calculator, and walked quickly out of his dad's study.

"C'mon, son, we don't want to be late," said his dad.

Standing by the door, Todd's mom handed him his lunch. He ran to the car. His dad backed out of the driveway and stopped.

"Son, I'll be right back." Todd's dad walked back into the house to get the answer sheet for Friday's exam. He returned to the car and drove about ten miles to Todd's school and his place of work.

During the drive to school, Todd couldn't think of anything else other than what he saw about a half an hour ago. "How can I erase answers, from my brain, to a test that I was not supposed to see?" he thought.

Todd tried everything he could to think of something else, but it was no use. He couldn't stop thinking about what he saw. His mom picked him up from school since his dad had to stay after school for a staff meeting.

"Hi, mom," said Todd.

"Hello, son, what's wrong?"

Todd settled back into a reclined position in his seat. As his mother drove away from the curb, he said, "I think I saw something I wasn't supposed to see."

"What do you think you saw that you weren't supposed to see?"

"I saw the answer sheet to dad's exam for the algebra test."

"Oh, my!" said his mom.

"I walked into dad's study, this morning, because I forgot my calculator. The answer sheet was right next to it on his desk."

"I see," said his mom.

"Now I can't get those answers to the test out of my head."

"Son it seems to me that it was an honest mistake. Your dad has always said he will never leave the answer sheet to his test just lying around because he doesn't want you to mistakenly see the answers to an exam that you have to take. Apparently, he made a mistake."

"But, mom, what am I going to do? If I take the test, it will be like I'm cheating because I already saw the answers."

"Todd, it wasn't your fault."

"Mom, dad knows that I don't know how to do those equations because he has tried to help me all week. If I take the test, I'm going to be torn between writing the correct answers, or not answering any questions at all."

"You know son, there is one wonderful thing that came from all of this."

"What could that be, mom? This whole thing has been a total disaster," said Todd in a disappointing tone.

"Well, I'm proud of you for doing the right thing."

"What do you mean, mom?"

"Even though you've seen the answers to tomorrow's test, it sounds like you have already made up your mind not to use them. I'm proud of you, and when I tell your dad, he will be just as proud of you if not more so."

"Aww, mom, you always told me that it's better to do the right thing the first time," said Todd smiling.

Needless to say, Todd's dad made a mistake. Some might even say he acted irresponsibly by leaving the answers to a test, his son had to take the very next day, on his desk in plain sight. While Mr. Stevenson is an adult, he is human and entitled to make his share of mistakes.

You might say that this entire episode could have been avoided if Todd was not in his dad's algebra class, or if his dad was more cognizant of his son's actions while he was helping him with his homework.

One could also ask the question, why didn't Todd's parents consider a tutor for their son? These are comments or questions that only Mr. and Mrs. Stevenson could answer. They could have some very good reasons to explain their position regarding these questions.

All parents have the freedom to make decisions for their children. They simply have to pray that the decisions they make are the right ones. After all, any decision made is considered the right one because it was made from the heart and with the right intentions in mind.

◆•••••••••••••◆

"Hey, Nathan, you wanna play some baseball? The sun is shining, and there's not a cloud in the sky!" said Nicholas, as he pressed the speaker button on his cell phone so he could tie his sneakers. "So, Nathan, you in?"

"Okay, Nicholas, I'll round up the rest of the guys, and we'll meet you at the park," said Nathan.

"You know, there's a girl who just moved into the neighborhood," said Nicholas. "I saw her trying to hit a baseball in her backyard. I might just teach her how to hit. I also might ask her if she wants to join us."

"I don't think that's a good idea. Girls can't play baseball!" said Nathan.

"Okay, well, I'll see you later," said Nicholas.

"What are your plans for today, son? It looks like it's going to be a nice day," said Mrs. Randolph.

"The guys and me plan…"

Nicholas' mother interrupted and said, "It's the guys and I. Now, we have been working on grammar all summer, son. Try to remember some of the things we've studied."

"Okay, mom, I will," said Nicholas smiling.

A parent should always correct her child's grammar whenever a teachable moment presents itself.

"I mean the guys and I plan to play baseball at the Camptown Park."

"Not before you have breakfast, son." Nicholas sat down to a hot breakfast of grits, eggs and bacon.

"Mom, there's a girl who just moved not too far from here. I see her whenever I ride my bike past her house. She's always trying to hit a baseball. I think I can help her, and I might even ask her if she wants to join our team. But, Nathan says girls can't play baseball."

"Son, it's never a good idea to judge someone. Always remember that. Besides, that girl may surprise you and especially Nathan."

Nicholas kissed his mom on the cheek, and pushed the screen door open. As he rode his bike down the street, on his way to the park, he saw his new neighbor trying to bat a ball in her backyard.

"She can't hit the ball at all. The bat didn't even come close. I'm going to go over there and show her how it's done," thought Nicholas.

As he rode up her driveway, the little girl came running down the drive to see who had stopped by.

"Hi, my name is Kiera. What's yours?"

Nicholas got off his bike, set the kickstand down, and said, "I'm Nicholas. I saw you trying to bat that ball, but it looked like you were having such a hard time. I thought I would come over and give you a few pointers."

"Oh that would be great," said Kiera as she smiled.

"Okay!" said Nicholas, as he picked up the bat and the two walked to the backyard.

"Alright, how should I hit the ball?" asked Kiera.

"Well, before I show you how to hit the ball, I have to show you how to hold the bat."

Nicholas lifted the bat to his right shoulder, as Kiera looked on.

"You wanna make sure you have a good grip here near the handle. Now, you try it."

Kiera took the bat, and put it on her left shoulder, and swung it around.

"Are you left-handed?" asked Nicholas.

"Yes, but, I can write with my left hand and my right hand."

"You know what that means? It means you can probably hit the ball while holding the bat on your left shoulder or your right," said Nicholas, as he picked up the plastic ball.

"Now, I'm going to show you how to hit the ball. With your feet apart, toss the ball into the air, and when it's almost even with your shoulders as it comes down, swing!" The ball landed over Kiera's backyard fence.

"I'll get it!" remarked Kiera, as she climbed the fence. Nicholas looked on.

"Boy, she sure knows how to jump a fence," thought Nicholas, as Kiera's feet landed in her neighbor's yard.

"I wonder if she was just trying to show off. She could have walked around," thought Nicholas.

"My turn!" said Kiera.

Nicholas handed Kiera the bat. She walked

over to her usual spot. With her feet apart, she threw the ball into the air. Waiting patiently for it, she swung. Crack, as the ball took off, and landed out of sight.

"Wow, that's what I call a hit!"

"Thanks," said Kiera.

"What are you doing this afternoon?" asked Nicholas.

"I don't know. I may read a book, and then watch a little television," said Kiera.

"How would you like to play baseball with me and my friends?"

"That would be great! I'll get my bike!" said Kiera.

As Nicholas and Kiera rode their bikes just inside the fence of the park, Nathan, Jerry, Simon, and Roger ran over to meet them.

"Who is she?" asked Nathan.

"This is Kiera, and I invited her to play baseball with us," said Nicholas.

"A girl can't play baseball," said Roger.

"You said it," added Jerry.

"C'mon, you guys. Let's give her a chance," said Simon.

"Okay, Simon, since you and Nicholas want her to play, she's on your team. Tell you what, I'll even let you guys go up first," said Nathan. Nathan has been the captain since he and Nicholas formed the baseball team two years ago.

"Batter up," yelled Jerry as he wound up his arm in an attempt to warm it up. Simon stepped up to the plate.

"A swing and a miss," said Jerry. Simon took a deep breath, and swung a second time.

"Strike two!" yelled Nathan.

"C'mon, Simon, you can do it," shouted Nicholas.

Simon dug his feet in the dirt, took a deep breath and…"Crack," the ball sailed through the air. Simon took off. He stopped at first base. Nicholas walked up to the batter's box.

"Okay, let's see what you got," said Jerry as he let go the first pitch.

Nicholas hit the ball a little further than Simon. He ran to first base as Simon ran to second.

"C'mon, you guys," yelled Nathan. "They can't score!"

Kiera picked up the bat, and concentrated on the things that Nicholas showed her.

"Feet apart, and wait for the ball," she said to herself.

Jerry let the ball fly, and a loud sound rang out. Simon had run all the way to home plate, as he watched the ball that Kiera hit fly over the fence. Nicholas walked all the way to home plate, but Kiera decided to jog, with an air of confidence, across home plate. Jerry was still shaking his head in disbelief.

"Let's see, that's three to zero," said Nicholas.

"I know, I know," said Jerry, as Simon stepped up. After the third swing, he walked over, handed the bat to Nicholas, and took a seat on the bench. Trying to encourage him, Kiera gave him a 'thumbs up.'

Jerry got ready, and Nicholas swung for the final time, as he dropped the bat because he struck out.

"Don't worry, guys, I'll fix it," said Kiera.

Jerry threw the first pitch, and Kiera did a repeat performance. This time, the ball sailed all the way, and landed just inside the fence. She took off running, as Nathan ran after the ball. But, it was too late. By the time he reached the fence, Kiera was crossing home plate.

Nathan calls Jerry and Roger over, and the three of them hold a conversation at third base.

"She sure can hit," said Jerry.

"She can run too," said Roger.

"What do you guys want to do?" asked Nathan.

"I think we should just admit that Nicholas has a better team," said Roger.

"Yeah, with that girl on his team, we can't beat them," said Jerry.

Nathan walked over to Nicholas to give him the news. "It looks like you guys win. We've decided to wave the white flag."

"I don't think we could have done it without Kiera," said Simon.

"You are so right," said Nathan.

After hearing her name, Kiera walked up to Nathan and said, "Good game, Nathan."

"It wasn't so good for me," said Nathan. "But, after today, I will never say girls can't play baseball because they can."

Kiera smiled, and everyone jumped on their bikes. "I guess mom was right. You can never judge a person, especially a girl," said Nicholas right in front of Nathan. Nathan just nodded his head.

7

Words or Leading by Example

Children have a pretty short attention span. They are not intrigued with a lot of words. Doing a whole lot of doing instead of doing a whole lot of words is far better for extremely young minds.

"Christina, how many times have I asked you not to eat any cookies before dinner? Eating just one cookie can fill your little tummy, and you may not want to eat your dinner. I know you had to climb up onto this chair to reach the cookie jar. How many times have I asked you not to climb onto the chair because you could fall and hurt yourself?" Mrs. Carson placed the lid onto the cookie jar.

"Hello, dear," said Mr. Carson.

"Hi, Christina! How's my little pumpkin doing?" he asked as he reached into the cookie jar. Christina looked on, but did not say anything. She simply thought, "How come Daddy can eat a cookie and I can't?"

"Hello, dear, we can all sit down to dinner in just a few minutes," said Mrs. Carson.

Later on, after Christina finished dinner and her mom helped her with her homework, Mrs. Carson asked seven year old Christina to go brush her teeth and get ready for bed. A few minutes later, Christina's mom walked into the bathroom and to a sink with toothpaste everywhere.

Mrs. Carson turned around, and walked into her daughter's room. In a calm tone, as she remembered having scolded her just before dinner, "Christina, dear, let's take a walk." Mom and daughter walked to the bathroom.

"Christina, Honey, what do you see all over the sink?" Before Christina could answer… "Hasn't your dad and I asked you to remember to wipe the sink after you brush your teeth, Sweetheart? Are you actually putting the toothpaste on your brush? Are you holding your mouth over the sink when you brush?"

"I try to do my best, mommy."

"Honey, that's all we ask you to do," said her dad having made his way up the stairs.

"Alright, Honey, you go on to bed," said her mom.

The next morning, Christina's dog, Champ, wandered into her room to awake her. He licked her arm. It was hanging over the edge of the bed. Having been a little startled, Christina sat up. She rubbed her eyes, and walked to the bathroom.

Walking over to the sink to wash her face, she saw traces of toothpaste on the sink. It wasn't quite as much as she spilled the day before when her mom told her about it. She wasn't sure who left the sink a little messy, but she was curious.

"How could mom say something to me about leaving toothpaste in the sink when it looks like someone did the same thing? I think I'll just keep this one to myself," she thought.

Mrs. Carson pulls into the driveway. She had just picked up her daughter from school. Christina jumps out of the car.

"Christina, remember to wipe your feet. It's quite wet out here. It rained all afternoon, and there are a few puddles on the sidewalk."

Christina was running so fast, she didn't hear her mom. She was trying to get to the phone before it stopped ringing. She ran around to the front door because she remembered her mom had waxed the kitchen floor this morning. She also remembered to wipe her feet before going into the house.

"Hello, hello!" said Christina.

The caller had hung up. Christina thought it might be her friend, Charlotte. She ran upstairs. By this time, Christina's mom made it into the kitchen carrying two bags of groceries. She took one look at the floor.

"Christina, Christina Carson. You come downstairs, and into this kitchen."

Christina knew that her mom was upset. Anytime she called her first and last name, it meant she could expect a good talking to. Christina hurried downstairs and into the kitchen.

"Look at this floor! I know I wiped my feet on the mat right in front of this doorway on the porch. I certainly didn't want to mess up this floor I waxed this morning. Just look at all of these smudges and dirt!"

Before Christina could answer… "I'm certain I asked you to make sure you wipe your feet before you come into this house."

"But, mom, I…"

"You may go to your room until it's time for dinner!"

Christina walked slowly through the kitchen that led into the living room, as her mom looked on. Her mom watched her daughter slowly climb the stairs. She wondered if she was too hard on her.

Just then, Mr. Carson was walking through the front door with some Chinese take-out.

"Hi, Honey! As you can see, you won't have to cook dinner. I left work early, and I came home to see if you had gotten dinner started. When I noticed that you had not, I decided to surprise you and Christina. I went back out for Chinese."

"Oh, since you were here earlier, you must have walked through the back door?" said Mrs. Carson, as she looked down at the dried smudges on the floor.

"Yes, and I forgot to wipe my feet," said her husband.

"I'm afraid I gave our daughter another lecture on wiping her feet before walking into this kitchen. Before carefully looking at the smudges on the floor; I just started in on our daughter. I guess I didn't bother to fully look at the smudges. I can see now that they are dry."

"Okay, Honey, I'll set the table, and you go on up and talk to her," said Mr. Carson.

Mr. Carson took some plates out of the cabinet, as Mrs. Carson walked the same path her daughter took just a few moments ago. She walked into her daughter's room to find her sitting at her desk reading a book.

"Hi, Sweetheart, I want to talk to you." Christina closed her book.

"When I was talking to you about making sure you wipe your feet before walking into the kitchen, you were trying to tell me something. What was it?"

"I wiped my feet on the mat by the front door because I remembered that you waxed the kitchen floor this morning," said Christina.

"I'm sorry, Sweetheart; I should have listened to what you had to say." Christina's mom hugged her daughter.

"So, mom, where did the smudges come from?"

"I'll let your dad tell you. Let's go downstairs. He's prepared a nice dinner for us."

While it is certainly a good idea to teach our children how to conduct themselves in various situations, perhaps it is better to lead by example. We have heard this saying many times. It does not only apply to academics where a teacher provides ways in which to solve problems, address a business letter, or design an electric car.

After explaining the do's and don'ts to your child, it's probably not a good idea to do what you ask your child not to do. Children learn by watching adults. They are extremely observant. They have a tendency to mimic what their parents do.

This is why it may be a little difficult to explain to a child how it's best to not go right when he sees you doing exactly what you ask him not to do. Simply telling your child that you can go right because you are the adult may cause your child to deliberately become defiant.

8

The School Bully

The idea of taking advantage of someone has been going on for years. It's a concept that can take on more than one form of ridicule. In the workplace, it's considered sexual harassment. In the business world, it's known as a corporate takeover. Infringing upon someone's rights within the school is known as bullying. While this term is more widely associated with children and teenagers, it can easily be linked to the previous scenarios.

"Okay, Honey, finish your breakfast. We have to leave for school in a few minutes."

Five year old Max was finishing his oatmeal when his mom walked into the kitchen with his backpack. He stood up, "I'm ready, mommy." Dressed in a short sleeve red shirt and black shorts, Max grabbed his backpack.

PARENT/TEACHER: A SIMULTANEOUS ROLE

"Here's your lunch, Max. Let's go."

Twelve blocks later, Mrs. Lawrence parked her car right in front of a tree next to Hamilton Elementary School. She walked around to the back door of the car.

Taking Max by the hand, the two walk up the steps and into the classroom. Max's mom stoops down,

"Okay, Max, I'll pick you up right here at 3:00 o'clock." Max's mom gave him a hug, and Max smiled.

As Max's mom walked away, Max could hear a couple of boys and girls snickering.

"Alright, let's go children," said Ms. Walker, as she closed the classroom door. She put the first assignment on the board, and instructed the class to begin work.

Max raised his hand to sharpen his pencil. On his way to the sharpener, he heard two students snickering and pointing as he passed by their desks. Max didn't say anything. After sharpening his pencil, he returned to his seat, and began working.

Hours later, the dismissal bell rang, and Max ran to where his mother was standing in the hall. Mrs. Lawrence took her son's hand, and the two walked out to the car. His mom opened the door to the back seat.

"How was school today, Honey?" asked Max's mom during the drive home.

"The kids were laughing at me."

"Why do you think they were laughing at you?"

"Billy was pointing at my shorts while his other hand was over his mouth. I think he was trying not to laugh too hard. But, he wasn't the only one. Sarah, Jimmy and Marsha were also snickering. I guess they didn't want Ms. Walker to find out what they were doing," said Max as he lowered his head, and looked really sad.

After pulling to a stop in the driveway, "Come on, son, let's go in, and I'll cut you a nice piece of apple pie."

"But, mom, you always said I couldn't have any sweets before dinner."

"Well, son, I'm going to make an exception today." Max wiped his tears.

A couple of hours later, Max's dad came home. "Hi, Max! Did anything special happen in school today?"

All of a sudden, Max jumped out of the kitchen chair and ran to his dad.
Mr. Lawrence could tell his son had been crying by the way he hugged him.

"What's wrong, son?"

"The kids, sniff, sniff, in my class, were laughing at me."

"Why were they laughing?" asked Max's dad as he sat Max in the chair right in front of his half eaten slice of apple pie.

"He said they were laughing because he was wearing shorts," said Mrs. Lawrence turning the chicken in the frying pan.

"Max, were you the only one wearing shorts on such a warm day?" asked his dad.

"Yes, dad, I was the only one wearing shorts. I heard Jimmy telling Billy that only babies wear shorts."

"Tell you what; let's try this tomorrow. Your mom is going to put another pair of shorts on you. If Jimmy begins to snicker, you raise your hand, and let your teacher know. Always remember to tell me, your mom and your teacher if someone is doing something that is not right."

The family finished their dinner, and Max's dad helped him with his homework.

The next morning, Max walked into the classroom with his brown shorts. Right away, Billy began pointing at Max. The usual crowd began pointing as well. Ms. Walker was putting the assignment on the whiteboard.

"MS. WALKER, WOULD YOU REPORT TO THE OFFICE, PLEASE?" Using the P. A. System, the school secretary had just summoned Ms. Walker to the office.

"Okay, everyone, please continue this morning's assignment on the board. Ms. Wright, will you monitor the class while I am in the office?" Ms. Wright is Ms. Walker's Teacher Assistant.

As soon as Ms. Walker was out of sight, Billy raised his hand to sharpen his pencil. Having gotten Ms. Wright's permission, he walked toward the pencil sharpener. As he sharpened his pencil, he began to snicker and point to Max.

Walking back to his seat, still pointing at

Max's shorts and snickering, "That's quite enough," said his teacher as she suddenly appeared in the classroom's doorway. "You march yourself right back to Max's desk and apologize to him."

"Max would you stand, please?" asked Ms. Walker. "Alright, Billy let's hear it."

"I'm sorry, Max," said Billy in a sincere tone.

"I accept your apology," said Max smiling.

Later on, "Hello, there, son," said Max's dad, as Max was coming down the stairs for dinner. "So, how did it go today in school?"

"Great!" said Max excitedly.

"He's been smiling and singing every since I brought him home from school," said Max's mom.

"Tell me what happened, son."

"I did just like you asked me to do, Dad. When Billy started laughing, I told the teacher. She made him apologize to me in front of the whooooole class, and he did!"

Picking Max up, "I'm so glad everything worked out for you, son," said Max's dad. Max simply smiled.

Being practical with your child concerning a problem he's having with a classmate is the first step towards an amicable solution. Max's mom decided against sending Max to school without shorts because this would have sent the wrong message. Children need to be taught how to solve a problem rather than running away from it.

◆••••••••••••◆

Nine year old Linda was experiencing a problem with another girl in her class. Marissa always met her by the gym door of Lakeside Elementary School every Monday. Linda doesn't know what to do. She was afraid to tell her mother, father and her teacher. She doesn't think the principal is going to do anything because he always has a few children in his office.

"Do you have my money, Linda?" asked Marissa as she hopped off her bike right in front of the gym door. Linda reached into her pocket, and pulled out a little handkerchief with seventy-five cents balled up inside.

"Thanks!" said Marissa, as she grabbed the handkerchief from Linda's hand. "I'll see you next week; same time, same channel," she said after chuckling. "You better have my money, and if you don't give it to me, I'm going to just take it since I won't have any lunch money," said Marissa. Marissa's dad can't afford to give his daughter lunch for all five days. Marissa rode off watching the empty handkerchief flutter to the ground.

As Linda's dad was pulling up to the school, he could see her pulling dandelions out of the ground. He drove right up to the tree and parked. Before he could get out of the car, Linda ran up.

"Hi, Sweetheart, are you ready to go?"

"Yes, daddy, I'm ready to go." Mr. Simon opened the door for his daughter as she climbed into the backseat and buckled her seatbelt.

"Is anything wrong, Linda?" asked her dad looking at his daughter's face.

"No, daddy, everything's okay." Linda didn't know how to tell her dad what was really going on. She was afraid that he would think it was her fault since she didn't tell him the first time Marissa asked her about her lunch money a couple of weeks ago.

Mr. Simon pulled the car into the garage. "Wait in the car, Honey, while I take the trash to the curb." Seconds later, Linda's dad opened her door.

"Okay, Linda, let's go inside."

"Hi, Sweetheart," said Linda's mom, as she took the backpack from around her daughter's shoulders.

"Honey, I'm so glad you called and said you could pick Linda up from school. I was running a little behind with dinner."

"That's okay, Sweetheart, Judge Harvey decided to clear his docket for the rest of the day."

Just then, Linda ran upstairs to wash her hands. "I think we may have a problem," said Mr. Simon. "We'll see what happens at dinner."

Minutes later, Mr. Simon poured everyone a glass of lemonade. "Okay, Honey, why don't you tell your mother and me what happened in school today." Both of Linda's parents knew something was wrong when Linda ran upstairs to wash her hands. She normally washes them downstairs whenever she comes home from school. I guess after two weeks of dealing with Marissa, Linda was becoming more and more upset.

"It's this girl at school!" cried Linda. "She

keeps telling me that she's going to take my lunch money every Monday, sniff, sniff. She said something about her dad not giving her lunch money on Mondays."

"How long has this been going on, Sweetheart?" asked Linda's dad?

"It started two weeks ago," said Linda drinking her lemonade. "I would take the money from my allowance you give me every Saturday."

"You mean it has been going on for two weeks?" asked her mom in a most concerned tone.

"Why didn't you tell us, Sweetheart?" asked her dad.

"I was afraid to," said Linda.

"Sweetheart, you must never be afraid to tell your mother and me about someone who is mistreating you, okay?"

"Yes, daddy, I will let you and mommy know."

"I think it's time for a day off from the office. I will drive you to school tomorrow, Sweetheart. You and I will stop in and see the principal," said Linda's dad.

"I think I'll go with you, dear. I'd like to hear what the principal intends to do about this."

"But, Honey, I thought tomorrow is your day to volunteer at the nursing home."

"I'll just have to call Marjorie and ask her to fill in for me. This is just as important."

The next morning, the Simon family entered the school office. "Good morning, we are Mr. and Mrs. Simon, and this is our daughter, Linda. We would like to speak with the principal," said Linda's dad.

"Good morning, Mr. and Mrs. Simon. The

principal will be with you in just a moment."

A minute later, "Mr. Fleming will see you all, now," said the secretary.

"Won't you all have a seat?" Linda and her parents sat together right in front of the principal's desk. "How can I help you?" asked Mr. Fleming.

"We'd like to know why a child in my daughter's class is bullying her and no one is doing anything about it," asked Linda's dad.

"I assure you, Mr. Simon, if no one is doing anything about it, it's because no one here at the school is aware of a matter such as this."

The principal turned to Linda and said, "Linda, did you tell anyone here, at the school, about someone from your class bullying you?"

Looking down, Linda said, "No, Mr. Fleming. I didn't tell anyone." Linda's parents looked at each other in amazement.

"Linda, Sweetheart, why didn't you tell anyone here at the school?" asked her mom.

"Because I didn't think anyone would believe me."

"Well, it appears that we, here at the school, need to be more cognizant of our children," said the principal.

"Yes, I quite agree," said Mr. Simon.

"Excuse me for a moment," said Mr. Fleming.

The principal put his finger on the intercom and said, "Ms. Johnson, I believe Ms. Hampton has a free period. Would you ask her to report to my office, please?"

"Yes sir," said Ms. Johnson.

A moment later, "Come right in, Ms. Hampton. This is Mr. and Mrs. Simon. I believe you know Linda." Linda's dad stood and extended his right hand.

"It's nice to meet both of you," said Ms. Hampton. "We haven't met before now because your daughter has never given me any problems. The parents I've met so far have children who've had some problems, and I've had to contact them."

"Linda, what is the student's name who's been bullying you, and what has this student done?" asked the principal.

"It's Marissa," said Linda clutching her mom's arm. "She has been taking my lunch money from me every Monday for two weeks. She said if I didn't give it to her, she was just going to take it."

"Ms. Hampton, what is Marissa's last name?"

"It's Thorndike," Mr. Fleming.

"Let's schedule a meeting with Mr. and Mrs. Simon and Marissa's folks for tomorrow. I'll leave it up to you to contact Marissa's parents."

"Marissa lives with her dad," said Ms. Hampton as she walked toward the door.

"Okay, well, you work out the arrangements," said Mr. Fleming.

The next morning, Mr. Thorndike and his daughter, Marissa, were walking into the office just as Linda's parents were getting ready to sit down.

"Mr. Fleming will see you all in his office now," said the secretary, as she was using the intercom to summon Linda's teacher.

"Won't you all have a seat?"

"What's this I hear about you accusing my daughter of bullying?" asked Marissa's dad in a rather rude manner.

"Let's wait for her teacher before we begin," said the principal. Just then, Ms. Hampton walked into his office.

"Alright, everyone, we are here to find out what's happening with Linda and Marissa, and to rectify the situation. Linda, I want to start with you. I want you to tell Marissa's dad what you told your folks and me yesterday here in my office," said the principal.

"For the past two weeks, Marissa has been taking my lunch money."

"You mean you been givin' me your money. I didn't take nothin' from you!" shouted Marissa.

"What do you mean…" started Linda's dad before the principal cut him off.

"Okay, okay, everyone settle down," said the principal.

"Now, Marissa, why would Linda give you her lunch money for the past two weeks?" asked the principal.

"I don't know. I guess she just wanted to," said Marissa.

"Okay, Linda, why would you give Marissa any money?" asked the principal.

"She said if I didn't give her my lunch money, she was just going to take it," said Linda.

"I've heard enough, Mr. Fleming. Those words, 'just have to take it,' are the same words my neighbors said she always uses when she tries to take things from the kids in our neighborhood," said Marissa's dad.

He turns to Mr. and Mrs. Simon, "I'm really sorry for what my daughter did. You let me know what the total is in all, and I'll make sure you get every penny back. Marissa, you march yourself right over to this girl's momma and daddy, and you tell them you're sorry. Then I want you to tell their little girl you're sorry, and that you are never going to try that again, you

130

hear?" said Marissa's dad in a firm tone. Marissa walked over and did as her dad had asked.

"I'm sorry, Linda," said Marissa in a somewhat kind voice.

"Okay," said Linda, as she reached for her mom's hand.

"I'm sorry Mr. and Mrs. Simon."

"Your apology is accepted, Marissa," said Linda's mom.

"Well, folks, I'm certainly glad we got to the bottom of this. Mr. and Mrs. Simon, are you satisfied with the results here today?" asked the principal.

"Yes, sir, Mr. Fleming, we are content with what has been said here today. We will let you get back to work so our daughter can get back to class," said Mr. Simon, as Ms. Hampton held the door open.

Mr. Thorndike took Marissa by the hand, and the two, along with Ms. Hampton, followed the Simons out of the principal's office.

"Linda, your dad and I will pick you up at the usual spot."

"Okay, mommy," said Linda as she walked down the hall to class.

Marissa and her dad walked right past Ms. Hampton's classroom. As Linda entered the classroom, she could hear the large door down the hall and near the front entrance of the school slam shut.

Parents should try to fully investigate a problem their child is having with someone in school prior to meeting with school personnel. Also, children should be taught to always confide in their parents, immediately, when something isn't right in school or any place else.

◆•••••••••••◆

Ernie Mason was carrying his usual five

books in one hand and a calculator in the other as he climbed the stairs of Alexander Middle School. He is one of the smartest kids in the school. He's known as Ernie the Geek. As he enters Mr. Nelson's algebra class, Ronnie says "Psst, hey Geek, can you help me solve the problem two plus six?"

"That's Mr. Geek to you, and the answer is forty plus sixty minus thirty minus sixty-two." Ronnie had the most baffled look on his face.

"Good morning, everyone, let's settle down. Open your Algebra books to page 219. Can anyone tell me the answer to number five?" asked Mr. Nelson.

"Ernie can. He knows the answer to every problem," said Ronnie in an unkind tone.

"That's enough, Ronnie," said Mr. Nelson.

"Ernie, I know that Ronnie was rude. However, would you like to show the class how to do number five on the whiteboard?" asked

Mr. Nelson.

"Okay, Mr. Nelson, I'll show the class."
After performing the problem, "The variable is
equal to nine," said Ernie.

"Very good, Ernie," said Mr. Nelson.
"Alright, class, I want you to finish this page for
homework." Upon hearing the bell, everyone
hurried to the door.

"Hey, Geek, you think you're so smart!"
said Ronnie, as soon as Ernie walked into the
hallway. Hearing this, the students who were
nearby walked right up to Ernie, and shielded
him from Ronnie.

"Hey, Ernie, don't mind him," said Michael.

"Yeah, Ernie, we're glad you're so smart,"
said Marsha.

"That's right," said Veronica. "I like the way
you help us."

"Ernie's a genius," said Matthew.

Ernie smiled. Even though he tries his best not to let Ronnie's comments bother him; he was relieved his friends appreciated his genius.

"Hey, Ernie, there's your mom," said Matthew, as they walk down the steps.

"Okay, I'll see you guys tomorrow." Ernie ran to his mom's car.

"How was school, son? Is Ronnie still making those unkind remarks?"

"Yes, mom, and I'm still trying to act as though they don't bother me."

"You know, son, Ronnie bullies you because he knows the answers come easy for you. He also knows that he has problems understanding the work from what you tell me. I have an idea. Why don't you walk up to Ronnie tomorrow, and offer to help him?"

"Awww, mom, he doesn't want my help."

"Maybe he doesn't ask you for any help because he's called you so many names, and he probably thinks you won't help him. But, if you show him you can be the bigger person by offering him help, he'll be so surprised you asked him, he just may accept your help. If he does accept your help, he may become one of your best friends instead of someone who wants to be a bully."

The next day, Ernie was walking down the hall on his way to class. He stopped for a drink of water near Ronnie's locker. All of a sudden, as Ernie drank from the fountain, Ronnie ran up and said, "Hey there, Geek!"

"That's Mr...." For a second, Ernie almost forgot what his mom told him the day before.

"Say, Ronnie, I want to talk to you about something."

"What do you want, Geek? You want me to

help you with your homework?" said Ronnie as
he burst into laughter.

"No, but I want to help you with yours."

"What makes you think I need help, Geek?"
asked Ronnie.

"Oh, I just took a guess," said Ernie in a
calm voice.

"Ok, why would you want to help me after
the things I said to you?" asked Ronnie.

"Let's just say, I'm trying to be a nice guy.
I'll meet you in the cafeteria at lunchtime, and
I'll work with you then," said Ernie.

A few hours later, Ernie was seen sitting at
the lunch table. He looked all around the school
cafeteria for Ronnie.

"Hi, Ernie," said his friend Matthew.

"Hi, Matthew. What are you doing here?"

"Ronnie asked me to give you this note. I'll see you later."

Ernie unfolded the piece of paper.

"Sorry, Geek, I just can't sit in the lunchroom while you help me with my homework. Too many people will be watching me. Thanks, anyway."

Ronnie

Ernie packed up his books, notepad, and walked into the hallway to see if he could find Ronnie. He didn't see Ronnie hiding just a few feet away behind a large trash can in the hall.

"He must really want to help me. He actually came into the hall looking for me. Starting tomorrow, I'm going to show everyone that the Geek, I mean Ernie, is okay with me," thought Ronnie.

The answer to the problem your child is having with someone who is considered a bully rests with your child turning the tables; so to speak. Consider the previous scenario as one of many solutions that result in your child allowing the other student to assume the responsibility he has created. Hopefully, your child's problem will result in a victory for him.

9

A Few Ways Children Learn

Children are taught the five senses between the ages of five and seven years of age. This exposure to the sense of hearing, sight, smell, taste, and touch can be introduced in a variety of ways. However, a parent can, for example, point out these senses by using the anatomical parts of her daughter's doll. Likewise, a parent can introduce this same concept using the anatomical parts on her son's action figure.

One or any combination of the three, methods of learning, kinesthetic, visual, and auditory can be used to assist a child, of any age, with learning concepts. The method of visual learning can be identified as a way in which a child navigates his way to understanding the lesson, as he may not quite grasp the concept through traditional methods.

A teacher may present a lesson without

targeting those children who learn best through visual mediums, touching manipulatives or simply listening. One size does not fit all, or all students do not learn the same way using one conventional method to reach every child.

Children can be fascinated with the art of drawing and coloring pictures. The use of visual imagery can aid in a child's understanding of various concepts.

◆•••••••••••◆

Mrs. Avery and her daughter are sitting in the family room. Mom is reading a story to five year old Kimberly. "Little Red Riding Hood" is one of the more widely known stories for children everywhere.

"…and that's the way the story of 'Little Red Riding Hood' ends," said Kimberly's mom. "Kimberly, I want you to be able to tell me what you remember about the very beginning of the story."

"I remember Little Red Riding Hood went

for a walk," said Kimberly.

"Very good, Sweetheart," said Kimberly's mom. "Now, where was Little Red Riding Hood going?"

"She was taking a walk to her grandmother's house."

"Honey, why do you think Little Red Riding Hood was going to her grandmother's house?"

"Can I draw you a picture to show you, mommy?"

"Yes, Honey, you may draw a picture."

Kimberly takes some paper and crayons from her baskets and draws a picture of Little Red Riding Hood holding a basket. She also draws a picture of grandma lying in bed.

Kimberly shows she understands the reason why Little Red Riding Hood went to her grandmother's house by drawing a picture of a basket. While she may not know how to verbally express the answer, she was able to draw a picture. This is an example of using visual imagery to respond to questions posed by the parent or the teacher.

◆••••••••••••◆

Three year old Jerry is having trouble writing the numbers three, four, and eight. His mom bought some modeling clay in an effort to help him learn to form the numbers correctly and have some fun doing so. The two of them are working at the dining room table.

"Here you are, son."

Ms. Richardson took a small, plastic bucket of different colored modeling clay out of the bag. Jerry picked up the blue clay and began to squeeze the clay between his fingers. Jerry's mom writes the numbers one through ten on a sheet of paper in a large format. Even though the numbers three, four and eight are the only numbers Jerry needs to work on, his mom wants to see if he can identify these numbers from the ten she had written.

"Can I make something, mommy?"

"Not right now, son. I want you to take some clay, and try to shape the clay so that it looks like the number three."

"Can I use any color?" asked Jerry.

"Yes, son, you may use any color you like." Jerry scraped the blue clay from his fingers, and looked at the numbers on the paper. He picked up the red clay, and molded the clay until he formed the number three.

"I did it mom, I did it!" His mom didn't have the heart to tell her son that the three was facing the wrong way.

"He worked so hard trying to make it just right. I can't very well tell him it's backwards," she thought. Jerry's mom knew that there would be time later to correct this minor detail. "For now, I think I'll just let him enjoy the moment," she added.

"Okay, honey, try to make the number four."

Jerry scraped off the red clay. After looking at the paper, he finished forming the number four.

"Nice job!" said mom, as Jerry scraped pieces of yellow clay from his fingers. "Alright, son, last one. But, before you start, what do you notice about the number eight?" Jerry looked at the number his mom had drawn.

"I know! It looks like two circles; one on top of the other."

"That's right, son." Jerry's mom intentionally drew an eight that reflects two nicely drawn circles. Her aim is to allow Jerry to do the same when he tries to draw this number.

Jerry scooped up some green clay. "I tried, mom, but my eight doesn't look like yours."

"That's okay, son. It still looks like an eight. Now, I want you to look at each number on this sheet of paper, and take your time to write each one." Jerry wrote the numbers one and two rather quickly. When he started to form the number three, he carefully formed the number eight.

"But, son…." Before his mom could finish, Jerry erased the left side of the two circles he had formed with his pencil. He continued writing the rest of the numbers.

"Nice job, son. You wrote all of the numbers correctly. I am so proud of you." Jerry's mom gave him a big hug. "How would you like to make some chocolate chip cookies?"

"Yeahhhhh….They're my favorite!"

"I remember," said his mom as they walked into the kitchen.

It looks like Jerry's got the hang of it. His mom used the modeling clay to ultimately help her son correctly write the numbers three, four and eight. The concept of learning through touch, or tactility, is one of the ways children can connect the dots; so to speak.

◆•••••••••••◆

"Mr. Livingston, after observing your son since the start of the school year, he appears to be a visual and tactile learner," said Ms. Gray.

"Can you be more specific?" asked Mr. Livingston.

"Michael Jr. learns best through visual imagery and moving or working with his hands. For example, one day, I engaged the class in a reading lesson. I read 'Goldilocks and the Three Bears,' as the children sat on the floor in front of me. I noticed, as I read through the story, using many inflections, Michael, Jr. was moving around on the floor. This may have been his way of listening to the story.

After reading the story, I asked the class to write three sentences to describe what happened in the story. Your son asked if he could draw a picture about the story instead. I said that would be fine. Mr. Livingston, children who prefer to use their hands to complete an assignment learn best this way. Drawing pictures was the best way for Michael Jr. to respond to this assignment. His learning style seems to include the use of auditory, visual and kinesthetic methods of learning, or movement, enabled him to complete the assignment.

"How interesting!" said Mr. Livingston. "Please, continue."

"As he was crawling about the floor, I could tell that his movement seemed to be in sync with the voice inflections I used as I read the story. His visual and kinesthetic methods of learning were implemented with his use of vivid imagery drawn and displayed with the pictures he drew based on the story."

Ms. Gray has emailed Mr. Livingston a schedule of weekly concepts Michael Jr.'s class will be introduced to during the month of October. Recalling what Ms. Gray brought to his attention about his son, Mr. Livingston uses Legos to introduce the first concept of length to Michael Jr.

"What do you want for your birthday, Michael Jr.?" asked his dad. Michael, Jr.'s birthday is a month away.

"I want a race car set with lots of tracks," said seven year old Michael Jr. excitedly.

"Alright, I tell you what; I've decided to prepare for your birthday a little early this year." Mr. Livingston went to the living room hall closet, and took out a large bag.

"Okay, son, I want you to sit right here at the table." Michael, Jr.'s eyes widened as his dad opened the bag and took out a pail of Legos, birthday party invitations, party hats, party streamers, and party horns.

"This month, your teacher is going to teach your class what is meant by length or how long something is. So, I thought we would use these

Legos and birthday things to help you understand what length means. By the time your teacher introduces it to your class; you will have a good understanding."

"Okay, dad, I'm ready," said Michael, Jr.

Mr. Livingston searches through the pile of Lego bricks and chooses twelve that are approximately one inch in length. He takes the measuring tape from the kitchen drawer, and stretches it to the length of a red Lego brick, as his son looks on.

Holding the Lego brick next to the measuring tape, Michael Jr.'s dad says, "See, Michael Jr., this Lego brick measures one inch. Did you see how I did this?"

"Yes, dad," said Michael, Jr., as he lowered his head closer to the measuring tape.

"Okay, son, I want you to take the remaining bricks from the pile and lay them end to end. But, I will lay out two, and I want you to lay out the rest." Mr. Livingston laid out two of the bricks, as his son sat eagerly awaiting his turn. "Okay, son, your turn." Michael, Jr. carefully laid out the remaining bricks from the pile.

"Alright, son, watch this."

Michael Jr. watched his dad closely, as he stretched out the measuring tape to measure the length of the line of Lego bricks.

"Now, son, this tape measures twelve inches or one foot. I want you take a party hat and lay it on its side. Then, I want you to measure the length of this hat from the tip to the end by laying Lego bricks end to end starting from the tip of this hat to the end of it."

Starting from the tip of the party hat, Michael Jr. laid out some Legos bricks from one end of the hat to the other. He went back and exchanged each brick with a different color just to make it colorful.

"Okay, son, how many bricks does the party

hat measure?" Michael Jr. counted the Lego bricks, and then stretched the measuring tape to make sure.

"It measures seven bricks, dad."

"Very good, son," said his dad.

The previous scenarios are examples of how children learn because they prefer learning in ways that are consistent with visual, kinesthetic, and auditory methods. Parents who want to know the way in which their children learn should consider these three mediums.

Visual learners have an eye for order. They want a bedroom that's free from clutter. Kinesthetic learners have a tendency to understand concepts that allow them to use their hands. For example, parents may encourage these learners to use their fingers to compute. Auditory learners respond best through verbal expressions, as in the case when Michel Jr.'s teacher read a story to the class, and he decided to move about the floor. This type of learner also doesn't mind chatting.

10

Siblings and Growth Spurts

Some parents can become concerned if one child doesn't seem as though he is as informed as his sibling. They may feel that given the siblings came from the same family, there shouldn't be any problems. Their children should learn to read, for example, at the same age.

"You know, Georgia, my sons aren't going to learn to read at the same age. But, didn't you say your sons didn't learn to read at the same time?" asked Janice.

"Yes, that's right, Jan. My son Mark learned to read at the age of six, and his sister, Diane, learned to read before she turned five years old," said Georgia.

"My son, Jonathan, learned to read and write at the age of five. But his brother, Leon, is not having much success at the age of six. I guess I expected him to at least learn how to read by the time he turned five years old," said Janice.

"Listen, Janice, children have what's known as "growth spurts," said Georgia.

"What's that?" asked Janice as she takes a seat, for this one, in Georgia's living room chair.

"A friend of mine told me about this a year ago. It's when one child somehow learns his ABC's by the time he's four years old. On the other hand, his sibling may not learn how to do these things until he's five years old. This is because the five year old hasn't reached his growth spurt. It seems a child learns at his own pace."

"Oh, I see. I just hope there won't be too big of a gap between my two boys," said Janice.

"It really shouldn't matter, Jan. A child masters what he can when he can. But, if you're that concerned, perhaps you could spend as much time as you can helping Leon work on those things that he may be having trouble with. Also, remember to have patience with your son," suggested Georgia.

◆•••••••••••◆

"Alexis, would you add this problem for me on the board?"

Alexis is in the second grade. Seven year old Alexis walked to the whiteboard, and tried to solve the math problem her teacher wrote.

The problem that Mrs. Grover had written has two addends with two digits in each one. As Alexis worked through the problem, her teacher said, "No, Alexis, you must add these two digits before you can write anything over here."

In a most sincere tone, "Has your mom been working with you while you do your homework?" asked Mrs. Grover.

"No, not really," said Alexis looking at the floor as the tears streamed down her face. "She always just tells me to go to my room and do my homework."

"Okay, I'm going to send another note home to your mother asking her to try and help you."

If a child senses that her mom doesn't appear to want to spend time with her and homework after school, she may get the impression that her mom doesn't care. Children can be very sensitive to things that matter the most.

Also, Alexis was probably embarrassed about not being able to work the problem on the board. She may even feel as though she is in this thing by herself. A child left to her own devices in order to navigate her way through learning may feel that there is no hope.

"Alexis, are you dressed yet? It's almost time for school," said her mom.

"I'm almost ready," yelled Alexis.

"I read the note your teacher sent home yesterday, Alexis. I want you to give this note to her as soon as you walk into the classroom. C'mon, let's get in the car," said her mom.

As Alexis walked into the classroom, she handed the note her mom had given her to the teacher.

"Mrs. Grover, here is a note my mom told me to give you."

"Thank you, Alexis," said Mrs. Grover, as she read the note.

Dear Mrs. Grover,

Alexis' brother, Christopher, can read, write and do math all by himself. He has been doing this since he started the First Grade. Since I didn't have to help him, Alexis should be able to learn just like Christopher did. I know that my daughter needs help, but I'm afraid I can't help her because I don't want to start something I can't finish.

I know I won't be able to do the math when she gets into middle school. So, it's probably best I don't start now. She'll come to expect more from me when she gets older, and of course I am in no position to really help her.

Ms. Spivey

"Alright class, I want everyone to take out their math workbooks. I want you to do problems one to ten on page fifty-seven," said Mrs. Grover.

"Alexis, would you come up here, please?"

Alexis walked to her teacher's desk. "Yes, Mrs. Grover," she said.

"Alexis, I read the note your mom sent me. I'm going to help her, so she can help you. Just before lunch, I will give your mother a call. You, along with your mother, and I will have lunch here in the classroom while everyone else is having lunch in the cafeteria. You may return to your seat." Alexis walked away with her head held high and smiling.

Mrs. Grover will inform Ms. Spivey, as she has already informed the parents at the very first meeting of the school year, that siblings have

varying 'growth spurts.' She'll go on to let her
know that a child learns at his own pace.

A teacher's willingness to assist a parent,
and a parent's desire to help her child, regardless
of the cost, is a partnership that can prove most
beneficial for any child.

Learning is the medium by which children
must entertain in order to ultimately become
successful in life. Again, it must begin at home
where parents are willing to invest the time to
work with their children. In doing so, they allow
their children to not only fare better in school,
but also enable them to realize that mommy and
daddy want them to do their best.

Children need a parent's firm hand of love
and guidance. This hand includes nothing more
than leading a child down the path of the many
explorations and wonders of learning that can
only be achieved through consistent parental
intervention along with a partnership with the
teacher. I can't stress enough how important it is
that this cohort is necessary if your child is to be

one of many who succeed in life as a result.

Acknowledgements

The success of a great book can only be made possible with the assistance of a person who wants to see you succeed as a writer.

My wife, Cassandra, has been a great support to me. As a retired elementary school teacher, she has provided me with much insight into the development of this completed work.

The wisdom of my Pastor, Bishop Robert E. Smith, Sr., also played an integral role in this completed work.

Made in the USA
Columbia, SC
10 July 2018